Marvel Chukwudi Pephel

The Barbershop Rhythm

Marvel Chukwudi Pephel

The Barbershop Rhythm

Poems

JustFiction Edition

Imprint
Any brand names and product names mentioned in this book are subject to trademark, brand or patent protection and are trademarks or registered trademarks of their respective holders. The use of brand names, product names, common names, trade names, product descriptions etc. even without a particular marking in this work is in no way to be construed to mean that such names may be regarded as unrestricted in respect of trademark and brand protection legislation and could thus be used by anyone.

Cover image: www.ingimage.com

Publisher:
JustFiction! Edition
is a trademark of
Dodo Books Indian Ocean Ltd., member of the OmniScriptum S.R.L Publishing group
str. A.Russo 15, of. 61, Chisinau-2068, Republic of Moldova Europe
Printed at: see last page
ISBN: 978-620-3-57875-1

THE BARBERSHOP RHYTHM

(Poems)

AUTHOR'S BIO

Marvel Chukwudi Pephel is a Nigerian writer who writes poems, short stories and other things besides. His poetry has won various prizes. His poem titled "Ogene" appears on 10,000 socks printed in Sweden and to be distributed across the world. He is the author of Nets Catching the Wind in One Fell Swoop and Christmas For Wide-eyed Monsters.

SYNOPSIS

The Barbershop Rhythm is a poetry chapbook that

comprises of 23 poems. The poems in the collection are

just plain masterful, if that's not to say the least. This is a

collection from a poet who is tirelessly looking for ways

to reinvent himself. It won't be a mistake to say that this

collection sees him pioneering a new form and

movement that could be called Rap Poetry. All the poems

in this slim collection are like punchlines and would leave

readers "chasing for the edge of the moon."

TABLE OF CONTENTS

- Basically I'm Saying

- Feels Like I'm Falling

SOMETHING NICE

Talk to me about something nice.

Like shucking corn and dancing nice.

About living right and dressing sense.

Talk to me about something nice,

Like different shoes and different size.

HOLLA, FELLAS IN FRANCE

Let's make some noise

And dance and bounce.

I CUT MY HAIR

What's your fee?

Ten grand or what, my gee?

A LOVER LOVER

Jilt my gee?

Oh, yes, Ofee!

I tell you truth.

A lover lover

Did jilt your gee.

And, oh, yes – O, yeah!

I tell you, Ofee!

Took his purse and stopped his pulse.

CHASING FOR THE EDGE OF THE MOON

I lost my life

And found it again

In a basin

At the bottom of the sea.

THIS YEAR, YEAH YEAH

Take my hand, Tennessee.

You can see, I'm busy.

Can't you?

Busy bee! I'm Bruce Bee!

Got you!

My hands are full this year.

Take this your eyes have seen.

'Cause no one knows really

If another chance shall ever come.

TIME BENDS

When you are having the time of your life.

Look at me – look at me, dear.

Talk one, talk two...

Say something.

Time won't bend your lips.

Darling, don't be afraid.

Laugh, dance...

Time won't bend your joy.

DEAD MAN LAUGHING

Jumping

Off and on

Off and on.

He puts his hand on his chin.

He smiles, remembers, chuckles.

Dead man laughing,

Jumping off and on

The board of fun.

SLOW CURTAIN FALLS

It still works

Even on a bad stage.

Slow curtain falls

Even in steelworks.

Slow curtain falls,

Even in life a big stage.

IN MOROSCO THEATRE, NEW YORK CITY

A magnum opus comes to life.

Beethoven's opus plays.

Broadway production will follow.

The audience claps.

The audience laughs.

A new child is born.

WIFE

If you have any difficulty obtaining a wife,

Try a fife

And love will flow with the rhythm of your life.

KEEP YOUR HANDS CLEAN

Let the chickens dance in dirt,

Let the pigs pout and snort.

You won't be the first nor the last

If you keep your hands just and

Clean.

THEY CALLED HIM BURNER BOY BECAUSE

He took a bursen burner

And cooked a bouncing dinner

On the Johnson Corner.

DON'T WORRY

Those in Warri

Are still worrying.

ASK SAPPHO

On the isle of Lesbos,

The women danced to lyre and calypso.

Two women kissed, laughing:

"I love you."

Don't clutch your heart, ask Sappho.

Ask Plato too.

The truth will surprise you.

WHY

Some people hurt their brothers.

Some people hurt their sisters.

And go about singing.

Why then would they bother

When they are sizzling

Or boiling in pots of doom?

BOOM SHAKALAKA

I box the skies,

I kick the bees,

I drown the seas.

Boom shakalaka!

I live like a prince.

Who? He!

I'm a velvety red wine, hehe.

I spill smooth vibes.

Who? He!

He, I!

And every day breaks upon a miraculous dawn stone.

OCTET

The stars are falling tonight

Like butterflies with dazzling lights.

And I am a man with colourful wings

Watching the Earth

With a lover's eye.

And the bats and the owls

Can't believe their eyes.

In North Ireland.

HAIR IN A COMB

I'm shooting for the grammies,

Yawning like my grannies.

Put me in my jammies

And lay me in Mercedes.

Like a hair in a comb,

Build me a room in a tomb.

Jam,

Jam jam and run

Like a man with a rum.

Oh, like a lair in a tomb

I'm a raccoon for the game.

ON RINGWOOD STREET

I put a hell of it.

They said, they said.

I still put a head of it.

The jerks, the jest...

I still put a chest of it.

On Ringwood Street,

I put a whole of it.

I ONCE LOVED A MONSTER

The monster ate my oyster.

But I'm Oersted who's been in Frankfurt.

So I picked a pitchfork

And forked myself through the monster.

And now, Oerstediggy I'm styled.

BASICALLY I'M SAYING

What you said and unsaid.

But you know how this saying thing goes.

That once it goes out of your mouth,

That it is far from hard

To find the unsaying elements.

But then who can take the heard

Into the well of the wild?

Who can convince the hard ears

To forgive and forget the heard words?

Basically I am saying, and saying

That I am not saying

Anything that has not been said.

FEELS LIKE I'M FALLING

Off, off

Like I'm falling

Off the coast

Like I'm falling

Off the wheels

Like I'm falling

Off the West

Like I'm falling

Funny, funny.

Contents

Printed by Books on Demand GmbH, Norderstedt / Germany